WHERE'S THE BIG DIPPER?

WHERE'S THE BIG DIPPER?

by Sidney Rosen
illustrated by Dean Lindberg

Carolrhoda Books, Inc./Minneapolis

Each word that appears in **BOLD** in the text is explained in the glossary on page 40.

Text copyright © 1995 by Sidney Rosen
Illustrations copyright © 1995 by Carolrhoda Books, Inc.
Photographs reproduced courtesy of: Alan Dyer, cover, pp. 2–3, 7, 34; NOAO, p. 5; © Robert C. Mitchell, p. 8; Al Belon, Geophysical Institute, University of Alaska, p. 9; Science Graphics, pp. 14, 29; American Lutheran Church, pp. 18–19; © Terence Dickinson, pp. 33, 37, 38–39.

Carolrhoda Books, Inc. c/o The Lerner Group
241 First Avenue North, Minneapolis, MN 55401

LIBRARY OF CONGRESS CATALOGING-IN-PUBLICATION DATA

Rosen, Sidney.
  Where's the Big Dipper? / by Sidney Rosen ; illustrated by Dean Lindberg.
    p. cm. — (A Question of science book)
  ISBN 0-87614-883-6
  1. Constellations—Miscellanea—Juvenile literature.
2. Ursa Major—Miscellanea—Juvenile literature.
[1. Constellations—Miscellanea. 2. Questions and answers.]
I. Lindberg, Dean, ill. II. Title. III. Series.
QB802.R67 1995
523.8—dc20
                                          94-39379
                                            CIP
                                             AC

Manufactured in the United States of America
1 2 3 4 5 6 – M – 00 99 98 97 96 95

Where can I find a big dipper?

Well, you can look in a kitchen drawer for a soup ladle. Or you can look up in the sky at night.

In the sky? What's a dipper doing up there?

The Big Dipper is the name many people give to a group of stars in the **northern hemisphere**. Together, these stars make a shape that looks just like a dipper. You can see the Big Dipper on most clear nights.

Oh, yeah. I see it! But how did people start naming star groups like the Big Dipper?

Long, long ago, people in places like China, India, Egypt, Babylonia, and Greece watched the stars in the sky at night. They imagined that the powers controlling their lives were all up there in the dark night sky. That's a pretty scary feeling, don't you think?

It sure is. But what did they see in the stars?

In some groups of stars, people saw the shapes of animals. In others, they could see the shapes of the gods of their myths. And a few more star groups, like the stars of the Big Dipper, looked like tools people used every day.

So that's how the Big Dipper got its name?

That's how it got *one* name. In other parts of the
world, it's called the Plow,

the Cart,

the Coffin,

or the Ox.

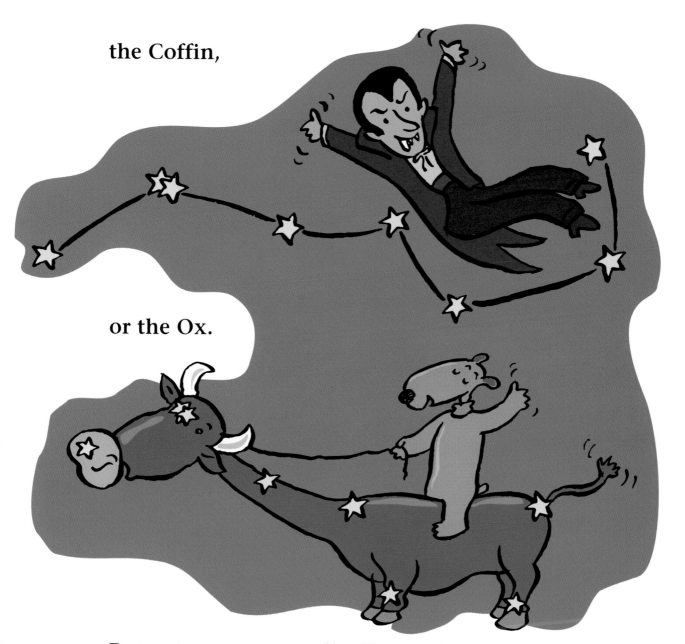

But **astronomers** will tell you that the Big Dipper is part of a larger group of stars called Ursa Major. That's Latin for "Big Bear." This group is what is known as a **constellation**.

What's a constellation?

It's the name given to a bunch of stars that move together as a group. The word *constellation* comes from two Latin words that mean "stars together."

Can I put stars together to make my own constellations?

Why not? Any night, when it is dark enough to see a lot of stars, pick out one group of stars that seem to go together. Then, just as if you were playing a dot-to-dot game, connect the stars. What does your star group look like? Give your constellation a name that fits.

Has anyone ever become famous for naming constellations?

Sure! Over a thousand years ago, Claudius Ptolemy, a famous Greek stargazer, counted and named 47 constellations.

Forty-seven! How did he ever keep track of so many?

Why don't most constellations look like the things they're supposed to be?

The stars in constellations are only white dots in the dark sky. Whether a constellation is supposed to be a bear or a dipper really depends on the imagination of the sky watcher. The outlines are just one more way to help us remember the constellations.

LIVE TONIGHT AT THE ACROPOLIS,

CLAUDIUS PTOLEMY, famous STARGAZER

Good question. In ancient times, people told stories about the different star groups to help remember them. For example, Andromeda, Cassiopeia, Perseus, and Pegasus are constellations that are all pretty much in the same part of the sky.

In the Greek myth, Pegasus is the winged horse Perseus flew on to rescue Andromeda, the daughter of Queen Cassiopeia.

What kind of story did they tell about the Big Bear?

The Big Bear started out as a woman named Callisto. She upset Hera, a goddess and the wife of the great god Zeus. The very angry Hera turned Callisto into a large bear. (Turning a person into a bear was not hard work for a goddess.)

One day, Callisto spotted her son, Arcas, out hunting. Like any mother, Callisto wanted to give her son a big bear hug. But Arcas wasn't happy to see a bear running at him. Just as Arcas was about to shoot Callisto, Zeus saved them both by changing Arcas into a smaller bear.

Why do the Little Bear and the Big Bear have such long tails?

According to Greek myth, Zeus stretched the tails when he threw Arcas and Callisto into the sky. But astronomers will tell you that both tails contain important landmarks in the night sky. In the Little Bear, the star at the end of the tail is Polaris, the star that points north. As for the Big Bear, the three tail stars (also the stars in the Big Dipper's handle) are among the brightest in the sky. The next-to-the-last star in the tail, Mizar, is really a double star. On a clear night, you should be able to see the two separate stars quite clearly.

To keep them from making Hera angry again, Zeus threw the bears, mother and son, up into the sky.

Wow, that's some story! But why did people bother remembering constellations?

They discovered that the constellations were useful.
First the ancient Babylonians and then the ancient
Greeks found that watching certain constellations
gave them a way of telling the time of the year.
Those constellations seemed to move across the sky
at night, just as the Sun did during the day.

They even moved along the same track as the Sun. That path or track is known as the **ecliptic**. There is one big difference between those constellations and the Sun.

What's that?

The ancient Greeks noticed that the constellations kept shifting a little every night. Every 30 days, a new constellation would begin rising in the east.

So those special constellations changed just like months on a calendar?

Yes. The Greeks counted 12 of them in one year.

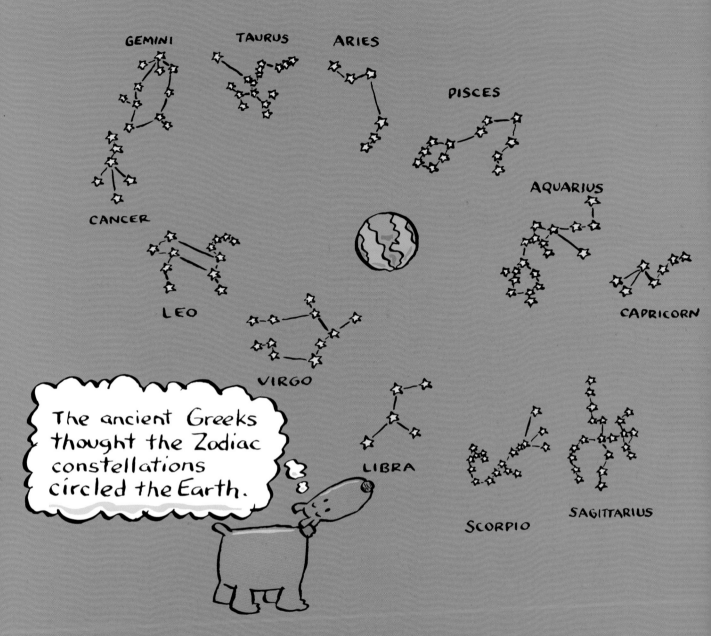

And they gave them a special name that we still use today. They are called the **Zodiac**. The name comes from two Greek words that mean "animals in a circle."

Do people still use the Zodiac to tell time?

Not really. Today we use the apparent motion of the Sun to make calendars. But the ancient Babylonians found another use for the constellations of the Zodiac.

What was that?

FISH

RAM

BULL

TWINS

WATER CARRIER

What are the Zodiac constellations?

Each of the 12 constellations of the Zodiac is known by its name in Latin and in English. They are:

Aries, the Ram
Taurus, the Bull
Gemini, the Twins
Cancer, the Crab
Leo, the Lion
Virgo, the Virgin
Libra, the Scales
Scorpio, the Scorpion
Sagittarius, the Archer
Capricorn, the Goat
Aquarius, the Water Carrier
and Pisces, the Fish.

CRAB

GOAT

LION

ARCHER

SCORPION

SCALES

VIRGIN

A kind of fortune-telling. They got the idea that in some magic way the stars affected people's lives. Whatever constellation of the Zodiac was in the sky when you were born determined what would happen to you for the rest of your life.

Wow! Is that true?

Are you kidding? This belief in the power of the stars is called **astrology**. Astronomers agree that astrology is *not* a science. They call it a **superstition**. That's like believing that carrying a rabbit's foot will bring you luck.

Are there many constellations that are not in the Zodiac?

Yes. Altogether, we recognize 88 constellations in the sky today.

Eighty-eight! How did we ever get so many?

Forty-seven were handed down to us from the
ancient Greeks. But the Greeks could only see the
part of the night sky that is north of the Earth's
equator. Most of the newer constellations were
found in the southern part of the sky.

*How did people decide on the new
constellations?*

How big are the constellations?

In general, the constellations in the northern sky—the ones we got from the Greeks—are fairly large. But the constellations in the southern sky are much smaller. For example, you could put five or six of the small southern constellations into the space taken up by Ursa Major, the Big Bear.

When European adventurers traveled south of the equator, they named many new constellations. By 1928, world astronomers decided that there were too many. They cut the number of constellations in both the northern and southern skies back to 88.

Were many of the old constellations cut out?

Yes, but not the very old ones, given to us by the Greeks. Three icky ones that were left out were the Leech, the Slug, and the Earthworm.

Today, astronomers use the positions of the 88 remaining constellations as a map of the sky, the same way we use a globe of the Earth.

So where's the Big Dipper on that map?

Well, you know that the Big Dipper is in the constellation called the Big Bear. But here are a few more tips.

In winter, the Big Dipper is near the northeastern horizon.

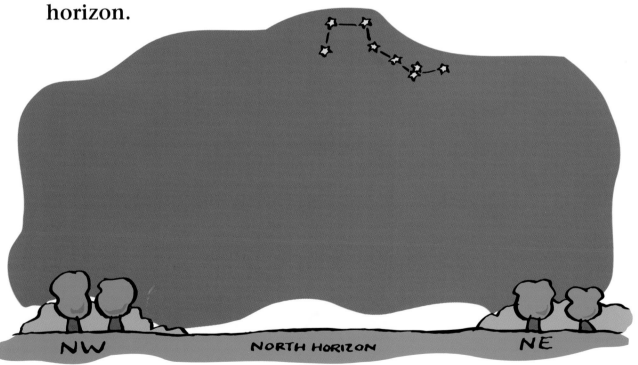

By spring, it has turned upside down and is almost directly overhead.

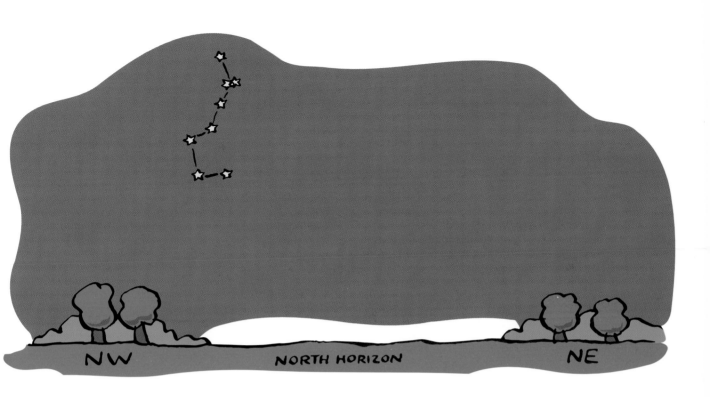

In summer, the Big Dipper is near the northwest horizon.

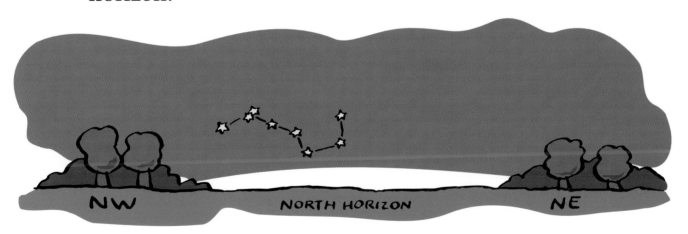

And in the fall, it's right-side-up again and near the northern horizon.

So why should I worry where the Big Dipper is?

For one thing, the Big Dipper can keep you from getting lost.

How's that?

The bucket part of the dipper has four stars. The two end ones are called the **pointers**. That's because they point to Polaris. Polaris is also called the **North Star**. It always points north.

How will that help me?

If you were a Viking sea captain a thousand years ago, the pointers and the North Star would keep you and your ship on course.

If you were an American slave in the 1800s, you could follow the North Star to states where slavery was against the law.

But will knowing where the Big Dipper is help me today?

Will I always be able to find the Big Dipper and the North Star?

Not if you live in Argentina or any other country in the world that's south of the equator. There, you should look for a constellation called Crux—the Southern Cross. This bright formation of four stars looks more like a kite than a cross. But if you look for either shape, you should be able to find it. Just as the Big Dipper points to the north for every sailor in the world, the Southern Cross points to the south.

Sure. If you are lost at sea or on a camping trip, you can always locate the north by finding the Big Dipper—and jumping from the pointer stars to the North Star. And you can use the Big Dipper to start star hopping.

What's star hopping?

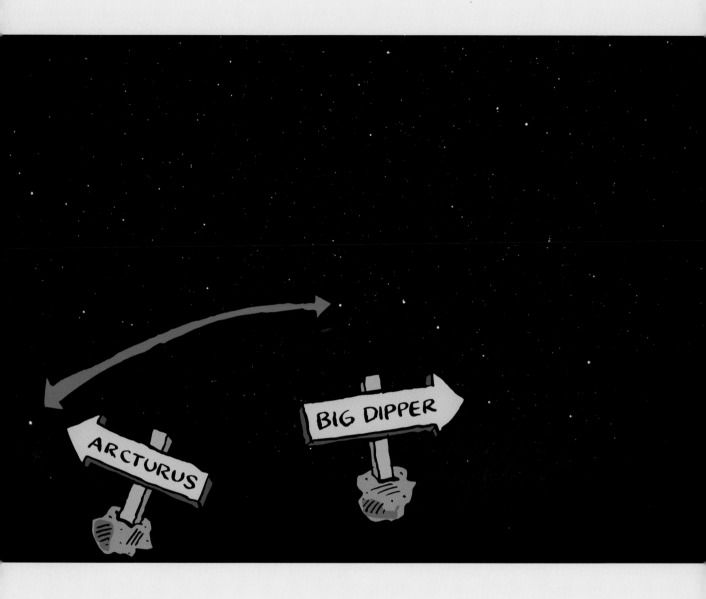

It's using stars you know to find another star or constellation. In the spring, for example, you can "hop" from the last star in the handle of the Big Dipper toward the eastern horizon. That will take you to Arcturus, the fourth brightest star in the sky.

Wow! Where else can the Big Dipper take me?

Wherever you want to go. Star groups like the Big
Dipper are landmarks in the sky. Astronomers use
the Big Dipper and the constellations to point the
way to unusual and wonderful sights.

Once you find the Big Dipper, look out! Your
journey through the stars has just begun!

GLOSSARY

astrology: The belief that the stars and planets control human lives and events on Earth

astronomers: Scientists who are interested in explaining how the universe works and who observe and study the planets, stars, and galaxies for this purpose

constellation: One of a number of patterns of fixed stars in the sky that are often named after animals, gods, or mythical heroes

ecliptic: The apparent path of the Sun around the Earth

equator: The imaginary circle or line that divides the Earth into two hemispheres, north and south

North Star: Also known as Polaris, this star is located at the end of the tail in Ursa Minor, the Little Bear. It points toward the North Pole.

northern hemisphere: That half of the Earth that is north of the equator

pointers: The two stars in the Big Dipper that form the outer edge of the dipper. Following a line of sight from these stars, you can find Polaris, the North Star.

superstition: A fear of the unknown that leads people to believe in magical ways of preventing bad luck and bringing good luck

Zodiac: The band of 12 constellations through which the Sun moves in its apparent path around the Earth